Hadean Eclogues

Hadean Eclogues

poems by

Frederick Turner

STORY LINE PRESS
1999

Published by Story Line Press, Inc.
Three Oaks Farm
PO Box 1240
Ashland, OR 97520-0055
www.storylinepress.com

This publication was made possible thanks in part to the
generous support of the Andrew W. Mellon Foundation,
the Charles Schwab Corporation Foundation, the Nicholas
Roerich Museum, the Oregon Arts Commission, the San
Francisco Foundation and our individual contributors.

Cover design: Lysa McDowell
Cover image: oil on canvas, "Landscape with a Specific View,
(Veritas, Utilitas, Venustas)," © 1988 David Ligare; Private
Collection, Greenwich, Connecticut.
Text design: Paul Moxon

Library of Congress Cataloging-in-Publication Data

Turner, Frederick, 1943–
    Hadean Eclogues : poems by Frederick Turner.
        p.   cm
    ISBN 1-885266-70-7 (alk. paper)
    I. Title.
PS3570.U69H34   1999
811'.54—dc21   99-22534
                                                        CIP

CONTENTS

Preface

Certain places on the Earth are hellmouths, gateways between the land of the living and the land of the dead. On this side of those gates the landscape is especially strange and beautiful; often it is a valley on the slopes of a volcano, like Virgil's Avernus in the shadow of Vesuvius, or the vale of Enna beneath Mount Etna that Milton compared to Paradise. Volcanic soil, fresh from the bowels of the planet, is famed for its fertility, and it can support rich harvests of corn and vine. Pluto, god of volcanoes, is god of money. But this place is also a place of danger; and at the hellmouth itself, the grass will not grow, and the ground is sulphurous, hollow, and bubbling with noxious gases. There must be a sacred precinct to demarcate the two worlds from each other, lest the living and the dead intermingle too freely. The Indians considered Yellowstone taboo for the same reasons, and would not settle there; and we do likewise.

It is the country that True Thomas discovers, after he has been abducted by the Queen of Faerie in the old Scots ballad of Thomas the Rhymer. He is carried on the back of her horse through the sunless country and across rivers of human blood to where the path divides in three—one to Heaven, one to Hell, and one to "fair Elfland." There they choose the third path that lies between the familiar ways of evil and good, the bonnie path that winds about the ferny brae, up the airy mountain, down the rushy glen. At last they reach the dark garden where seven hundred years can pass in seven, and he receives from the queen the very awkward gift of truth-telling. (How, he asks, can I prosper in the market or avoid the wrath of a king if I have this gift—and how can I speak to a fair lady if I must always say what is in my mind?) This is the country of the dead, but also of the ever-living: the Western Mountain of the Chinese, the Babylonian Dilmun, the Happy Hunting Grounds of the Plains Indians. It is also the land of certain dreams, unbearably delicious, but lit always by a strange anxiety, an edge of fear at the unknown, an urgency of unknown cause. It is a place both of the past and the future; it is the dream you have of a house you once lived in, and in the dream you are so happy and at home there, and just before you awaken to find it is lost and gone forever, there is a special moment of yearning, an opening to something even deeper, that is brushed swiftly away by the return of consciousness.

These poems come out of that place. An eclogue is a sort of picnic in words, a *déjeuner sur l'herbe,* and they are little picnics beside the cavern-mouth of Hades, the underworld. They are eclectic eclogues—their classicism, the classicism of the twenty-first century, is not an exclusively European one or even a Western one, but a classicism that their poet thought he found in his conversations with shamans, living and dead, from every corner of the world. The formal meters in which these poems are composed are the medium of that conversation; they are the way I listen to voices other than my own.

Where is the hadean arcadia of the twenty-first century? Ancient poets always found it in the countryside, in a pastoral place where the cultivated mingled with the uncultivated, or in sacred groves that were uninhabited but managed unobtrusively by eccentric sibyls or priests. In the nineteenth century they found it in the wild landscapes, or what they thought were wild—in the desert, the Alps, the Lake District, the exotic lands of Abyssinia or Xanadu. Thus their attitude to it was elegiac, as they foresaw the encroachments of the city, the dark satanic mills. In the twentieth century they found it in the city, where the evening is laid out on the sky like a patient etherized upon a table. In the twenty-first century we will find it in the suburbs, in a suburban *Rus* that is not so far away from the arcadia of the bucolic poets, of Virgil and Horace, Tu Fu and Li Po, Kalidasa and Hafez, Radnóti and Pasternak. But it is a post-technological landscape, one in which the technology is perfecting itself into invisibility, and where form has ceased to follow function but rather elaborates itself into new, delicate, intelligible structures that create new functions—functions that we suddenly recognize from the cultural past. There are times when the present breaks the shackles of the past to create the future—the modern age, now past, was one of those. But there are also times, like the Renaissance and our own coming twenty-first century, when it is the past that creates the future, by breaking the shackles of the present. The environmental restorationists are recreating extinct ecosystems—prairies, oak openings, dry tropical forests—on land once apparently claimed forever for the city or the farm.

In North Texas, where I live, there is strange zone of savannahs, residential real estate and huge artificial lakes, very tangled and unkempt in places (and then suddenly tamed or as suddenly let go wild again), where a whole new ecology is evolving—plant and bird species from Louisiana, the eastern forests, the Gulf Coast, the Yucatán. The floating islands of the old Aztec Tenochtitlán before the Spanish came, in the suburban district of Xochimilco ("the land of the flower gardens") must have been such a place. There are territories below sea level, like the polders of Holland or the shores of Galilee, deep beneath imaginary oceans, where the light is just so, the light of the planet Mars when we have turned that desert into a dimly-lit arcadia. Seashores and springtimes sometimes show it, when the sunlight is at a low angle and the evening lengthens out after the clocks have been set forward.

This theme-park place, this Disneyland of the dead or everliving, where Orpheus, Aeneas and Dante have their adventures, has its detractors. It is in doubtful taste, indeed it is kitsch, for its irony is aimed not at itself but at the censoriousness of its critics. It gently mocks the one-way linear equations of morality and power that are so dear to the political culture. It is the domain of nonlinearity, of dissipative systems that flourish on the flow of decay, of perverse consensual fetishisms, of emergent structures and fractal depth; it is drawn by strange attractors rather than pushed by causes and laws. It recognizes power and beauty as opposites, and chooses the power of beauty.

The hadean arcady is also a place of religious experience. But in the twenty-first century it will be one in which the difference between existentialist-atheist descriptions of paradise, and Judeo-Christian ones (or Buddhist, Muslim, Hindu, Mayan, Taoist, or Aborigine ones for that matter), will have begun to go away. Suppose there could be a poetry, even a scientific description of reality, that left undamaged the principles, the honor, the history and myth, the ritual, the intellectual criteria of believers and unbelievers of all kinds alike—as long as they were people of depth and thought and imagination? This is the language that poets must seek now, not for the sake of political harmony but because no other imaginative challenge is half as interesting, no other project requires so complete a subjection of the poet's ego to the wayward and terrifying spirit of human language. What if there might be a death mass for *human beings*, not just Catholics, or a science-fiction quantum-temporal "explanation" of the life of Christ that discovered by formal poetic means a deeper respect and love for Him than any pious account? What if the Mayan concept of the fertile zero, expressed as it might have been in human sacrifice and elaborated in the death-cults of the Aztecs over a thousand years later, might be the missing piece in both Christian theology and cosmological physics?

Hadean Eclogues

Winter Evening in Texas

On a field of velvet night
Float a sheet of violet glass;
Light that glass with rosy light
From beneath, like bronze or brass;
Carelessly then let a drop
From the white-hot pot of Being
Splash upon this tabletop
Brighter than the power of seeing;
Let it form a crescent moon
With a spilt point, for a star;
Then set crimson flames to swoon
Where the darkened woodlands are.

Texas Eclogues

One

Now there's a pause in the journey, the journey to carry the epic,
Carry the good news, the future, to those who have almost forgotten:
Episodes out of the story, not told because not important,
Not in the line of the argument, remembered nevertheless.
Consider the prince in his exile, his grief, his constant anxiety,
Constant inner euphoria; dreaming, addicted to dreaming,
Waking among the farmers, as a woodcutter earning his bread
Incognito, known only to one or two faithful disguised counsellors,
Just so am I, the deposed one, the king hiding out in the country,
Mad duke, sly fox missing a foot from the trap, the escapist.
Just so I have been dreaming, plotting the means of my triumph,
Waiting in silent joy for the time of my fresh revelation,
Chuckling and waiting, the craziness sometimes too clear in my eyes, too
Obvious, seen in the scrap of mirror I packed in my exodus.

This is the landscape that nobody wants. It's my cup of rejection:
Driven to this unformed scraggly ignored backlot, this not-quite
Prairie, not-quite thicket, not even natural corner of
Texas, the hardscrabble left butt of a demoralized nation,
It is my choice and my pleasure to cherish this haphazard wilderness.
No, it's not even "wild"—it's a neglected product of artifice.
Come, let us walk by an improvised lakeshore, be given a vision:
Beaches of black dust, beautiful white ghosts, this drowned forest.

Two

I walk by Lavon Lake in the Indian summer,
By the satiny-silver bones and skulls of the trees,
Where I find half-buried in crumbly sable gumbo
The great greenblack shell of a dead snapping turtle,
A tiny convolvulus, violet-throated, enweaved
In its gaping orifice; a foam-rubber cushion choked
With the lake-silt, bearing a miniature garden of clubferns,
An ant's-nest, a gauzewinged azure surefooted dragonfly!
The caked and powdery beach is curiously pure:
Even the halfburied Budweiser gleams in the sungold,
And bronzy-black grasshoppers evolve to scavenge this newness,
And archaean footprints of North American marsupials
Cross with the dog's, the crane's thin cuneiform
Stalked by what must be the paws of a feral cat.
The seeds of willows have made their way here, have grown
Into little sallowy arbors of halfshadow green
Where the shore is spongy, prairie aquifers spring
To the surface, lagoons with tussocks of buffalo-grass,
Groves of exotic bamboo, impede the footsteps.
And the lake, lit by the glowing skeletons, green
In the unnatural light of my sunglasses, turns to light blue
And mirrors, fantastic, the miniature hills of the shore,
Gold-brown in the early fall, with woodlands,
Radio-beacons, real-estate development.

How young the world is. I am its oldest inhabitant;
I was there at its white condensation, I am here, I shiver,

I hear overhead the whimpering whoop of the geese,
Two-year-old ghosts of this, the new dispensation,
In their plunge southward over the edge of the planet.
They do not know where they are going; I drink them,
Swallow their great raggedy flightline into
The inner sky of my spirit, the divine southland
That dreams in the web of the human software, the fold
That the shepherd has made by the side of the still waters.

And the sky is so blue! The outlines but not the substance
Of brilliant clouds sometimes appear in its firmament,
Deflecting the sunrays to cast a shadow of azure
Over the breezed, hazy perfection of heaven.
This place of bones is a province of ancient Pangaea;
I am the large land mammal of the Pleistocene,
My food is the turbulence caused by the jut of consciousness
Into the flow of world-information, the swirl of spirit
Boiling about the point where nature, transfigured,
Breaks and shivers into the glow of the supernatural.

Three

It was the dreams that brought me to this place.
Always I wandered stranded in a strange land,
And found there heart-constricting beauties, hills
With brilliant landslip-scars, and evening cities,
And foreign railway-stations, and a coast
Deserted, forested; dark estuaries,

Shining lagoons, and roaring tideraces;
But the great task, the journey, called to me,
A journey I could only start from home,
And I was lost, could not find my way back,
And every effort only drew me deeper,
And how was I to know I'd not begun
The task already, but the drug of sleep
Had choked the memory of what it was?

It was at that time I began to walk
Restless over this disregarded Texas,
Always avoiding, though, the dammed-up lake,
Which was defiled in my imagination
By the hand men had had in its first making,
And then I always feared its tree-bone forest.
But one hot day I found a dried-up creek,
Whose bed was muffled clay, where cottonwoods
Closed in a spacious winding passageway
Of brown and lukewarm shade that afternoon,
And all about the ground was glowing green
With a strange weed whose fruit was a green lantern,
Papery thin and airtight like a drum
That popped when trodden on, and in this field
Of hadean shadow-fruit so insubstantial,
Multitudinous, and phosphorescent,
Mesmerized, I could not leave the way,
And many miles I must have wandered on,
While through the trees sometimes a little sky
Seemed to suggest some huger open space,

Mysterious, beyond the ordinary world.
And the long carpet of the greenish lanterns
Still drew me on, over the fallen timber,
Over the carcass of an ancient Ford,
Trapped as a man is trapped within the journey
Of his life, trapped by his strength as much
As by his imperceptible weakening,
And a soft drumbeat drives him on, his heart,
His destiny, even the dark addiction
To reckless loss that is the ache of being.
At last the gloomy passage opened out
Into a wide waste of barren ground,
And the light blazed through the backlit leaves
Of willows that would part before my hands,
And now I stepped out on the sunlit shore,
Eyes dazzled by the molten mirror-light.
And there it was. These ponded tons of water
Seemed like the last years of my mortal life,
Stored in their half-mysterious and drowned grottos
Behind the dam of discipline and pain.
I blessed the lake then, and in that very moment
It seemed the wall of trees shattered and broke
With a great crack and creak of snapping timber,
And from the leaves burst a gigantic bird,
Dark as the thunder, and as it flew it croaked
And its huge shadow fled before it on the water.
This thing I knew was dream kin to my soul.
I need must follow if I would be whole.

Four

Another summer, I sought the glade of persimmons
Where like a dream I was nourished by fruit from the tree;
But in rank new growth I soon became quite bewildered;
I never could find my tree, but pushed on blindly
Till a great thorn thicket had utterly surrounded me.
And the cruel heat increased in its airless subways,
And, lightly clad, I was torn by the long brambles,
And the fire ants swarmed on me whenever I stood still.
I have held my guard on the fighting-floor ringed by opponents,
But now I was weeping sick, and weary, and disgusted,
And but for the itch and the pain, could have sat down and died.
And how I escaped the place I really do not know.
I must have just forced and ripped my way on through;
I had a stick of driftwood and smashed at the trailing thorns,
And I cursed and I cursed at the rank stupidity of it all.
Help must have been barely a mile away.
I could have gone back; I was not lost but entrapped.
But the thing had revealed to me something that seemed a reality:
Were I a child the place would have had no mercy,
When I was lost in the forest in Africa I could have died.
The world's not designed for the comfort of us, its masters;
The Earth itself is lost in the thickets of darkness,
In the thickets of hard radiation, in the thickets of fire.
And we are such tenderfoots, bien-pensant strangers, hostages.
And even when I had escaped, I felt all around me
The thorns of the desert, the ants that devour the soul.
And it's no consolation that the lake and all its ecology,

Its forests and swamps and terrible tangled places
Were all brought about by the clever hand of mankind;
That our shining machines, our armor, our starry ambitions
Can shape to a garden the wastelands that we inherit;
For the thorns, the quicksands, the ants and the ruthless sun
Are rank and rooted through all the shores of the mind,
And grow without maps in the veins of the human heart,
Where there's no chain or blade to tear them away;
And even your wife, your child, your oldest friend,
The fruit-tree arbor you seek through all of your life,
Are matted and dreary with death and the tangles of time.

But something else needs to be said, and it's not just whistling.
Crouched in that dreadful room, whose low roof was thorns,
Whose floor was the soft soil-heaps of formic-stink ants,
And wound about by the strings of the thorns, like a Gulliver,
I felt the pressure of being, outside me but also
Within me, and two balls of blinding fire
Beat on that thicket: the sun—and the orb of the brain.

Five

Once, beside the shining water,
All my years fell from my shoulders;
Mud-besmirched from boots to eyebrows,
I, a boy, got out my penknife,
Cut a staff to help me balance,
Cut a noble alder sapling,

Fine and straight like boyhood passions,
Trimmed it of its leaves and branchlets,
Felt its length and rodlike stiffness.
Later, by a bamboo thicket,
I remembered bamboo arrows,
How they could be fletched with feathers,
How they could be armed with warheads,
So I cut five green bamboo-shafts.
What could serve to string my weapon?
Fishing-line is sometimes tangled
In the driftwood at the margin,
Both a nuisance and a treasure;
Now, of course, I could find nothing.
But a shadowy Great Blue Heron
Broke from cover, clapped the water,
Glided out across the shining;
Where he'd roosted, there were feathers —
Crispy, with a blueblack glitter.
They would stabilize my arrows.
Inland, then, I sought my bowstring;
Junipers, with pale blue berries,
Crept their roots across the limestone;
One I ripped up from its crevice,
Would not part until I cut it,
Made a serviceable bowstring.
Now I worked upon my arrows:
Cut and splayed the pliant wicker,
Bound a flint into its cradle,
Split one end and set the feather,

Nocked the butt and tied it tightly.
Then I strung the bow; it bent,
Held the string upon its notches.
Bows when strung are light and heavy;
Bound within your palm electric,
Ask the hand to set the arrow,
Ask the fingers to encurl it,
Ask the shoulderblades to open,
Call out for a living target.
So I raised the bow; the heron
Perched upon a distant treelimb;
Then I turned, and shot the arrow
Harmlessly against a fencepost,
All the technical endeavor
Being target quite sufficient.
For the arrow flew unswerving,
Driven by that ancient gesture,
Hand sustaining, hand relaxing,
Fingers loosed to loose the impulse,
Boy and early human hunter
Now commuted to a poet
Playing by a shining water.

Six

And once, in early March, I found a spring-fed pond
Blown to a passionate and inky blue
By a warm wind that bent the heavy bullrushes.

A swale of Indian grass shone in the sun
Turning, as the wind waves ran through it, apricot
And pink and faintest buffs and bays and tawns.
The water, cold and volatile, was clear on down
To secret navels, weed-ways, velvet green,
And yet the rippled surface, cobalt, pure, remained
As perfect in its color as a gem.
The margins boiled with sources, flowed with springs,
As if a bosom pumped a constant blush.
These little lakes are new; the airline passengers
Who, in the long glide to the Dallas airports
Set aside newspapers and stare at the crimson dusk,
Can see a thousand mirrors made of blood.
How does this earth's emotion well up so untrained?
What pressure drives the limestone aquifers?
Only the poet who has walked the shades can say,
Only the hadean and learned poet.
It's not the winter rains, it's not the thick black clays;
Nature unsouled of humankind cannot
So make its clear lymph spout from all its pores and wells.
The great reserves, dammed for the city's thirst,
So weigh upon the land, so swell and prime its prairies
That perforce this clear milk shakes out upon
The white lime glacis of its hills, and drowns its meadows.
Nature's our body, which we've disciplined
Wellnigh, no doubt, to death by our diasporas;
But there will come a time when human love
Will run through all the planet's veins and caves.

The Cold Applause (Maine, 1989)

Some tempest cast this wreckage of a jetty,
A forestage for an audience of waves,
Upon the headland's cyclopean stones.
Its boards are satin-grey with bitter salt
And bone-dry with the floodlights of the sun.
But now a shy wild rose has stepped onstage,
Her blanched white face suffusing with a blush.

Villanelle on the Oregon Coast

For Margaret Prentice

Many a time I've dreamed of such a place,
Where darkened headlands tumbled to the shore
And a white ocean blew against my face;

An inland valley gave a breathing space
Against the water's overwhelming roar.
Many a time I've dreamed of such a place,

But the great wind of dream-time would erase
All human detail, leaving just a core
That the white ocean blew against my face;

Now, though, our footprints measure out our pace
Upon this homeland that I never saw
(Many a time I've dreamed of such a place);

The cypress-pins and huckleberry-lace
Had been invisible to me before
When the white ocean blew against my face:

Sister and stranger, you gave me the grace
To read the print upon the windblind shore.
Many a time I'll dream of such a place,
Where that white ocean blows against my face.

Revisiting Northamptonshire

The spring is checked in this unnatural chill.
As if a bowl of cold pent up the year,
Its lifebirth stands eternal, glassy, still,
The buds anatomized as they appear.

The may, refrigerated, blooms in June;
The chestnut-candles cannot fall or die;
The yellow fields of mustard, in a swoon,
Make an inverted, dazzling, heatless sky.

Sequence is both suspended and preserved.
The tiny flowers of early spring survive
Into regimes they've never known, unnerved,
As if in terror that they're still alive.

And I, the traveller, have ventured here
Armed with the paralyzing strength of man,
To where I was a child as helpless-dear
As these white blossoms where my life began.

And is the glass of human memory,
This little draught of immortality, the drug
That holds the world in immobility
Against the pathos of its living tug?

Do I, a cruel nor'easter, freeze the spring,
Compel this frigid heaven on the earth?
And when I turn away, will everything
Breathe freely once again in its rebirth?

Pear Tree in March

First comes the white of desire,
Then comes the living green.
But today it's a greenwhite lyre,
Neither one nor the other: between.

Geysers in Yellowstone

Streamers of steam go galloping over the pinebarrens;
Banners of shredded cloud, white, windborne,
Pour through the passes, blow by the blueblack ridges,
Make them to vanish, reappear like islands in airsea—
All of it fine, clear, thousandmile distant,
Yet *here*, inbreathed through the anguished and laboring
    nostril
In longdrawn streams of thinwine, quenchingless air.
And the earth gasps through its blowholes, it grunts in its
    messes,
Its messes of turquoise and coral, viridian vernissage,
Its caverns of aqua, its vulvas befringed and envirgined
With pure dazzlewhite bristles of gypsum and calx,
Then groans, its quivery torso blanched as an invalid.
This is the land of the dead, the hadean arcady.

You shiver, a scatter of snowscour spins through the
    gladeland,
Three badges of sunlight climb up the mountainside,
And suddenly now you can smell, as if locks in your head
Were unclenched, the resinous weeps of the pine and the
    juniper,
The char of the pith and the bark, the hell of the burning,
The waft, the lukewarm yeasty blast of the sulfur;

And, drawn by the heat of the steam, you sink to your
    elbows
Your long, yellowing arms in the brew of the water
As clear as the springlight, and a bolt, an electrical shock
Shoots from your wrists to the deepest sinks of your body,
Its hidden stanchions and cisterns, and you are undone.

Columbia Runs a Temperature

Those monster-states that held the world in fear,
Sloughing the dead nations they had sucked dry,
Have found a place to lay their eggs in: here.

And now I am so weak that I could cry.
I am defeated. All my strength was spent
Wrestling in darkness with their nine-faced lie;

And when their wall and blood-drenched battlement
Had fallen, then I thought my work was done,
And I once more could seek enlightenment;

And take the old path of the evening sun
Along the forest-edge, the meadow-mazes,
To where I knew the river had to run.

But now I see the sickness in their faces,
The cold envy of any sexual gift,
The shamed self-righteous screaming of the races;

My body's torn with each new-fangled rift,
Chiefly within the head that is its school,
Where the disease is feverish and swift.

This land's the body, and I am the soul.
I am sent here to fill the hills with nerves,
To take the pulse of every molecule.

My people are those quick electric nerves:
They are my ganglia and sensorium.
It is the flesh that cries, the god that serves.

Yeats feared that innocence was drowned, and some
Thought him an old fussbudget to complain:
The rough beast, as he said it would, did come.

The best lack all conviction, now as then.
My poets cower and will not tell the truth.
Within my guts the beast has grown again.

I will remember the fresh strength of my youth,
When I struck through the snows of Germany,
And dared the monster's claw, the monster's tooth,

And laid the chambers bare for all to see,
And in the cold air of the soldier's myth,
Made history a work of poetry.

The Bruges Virgin

The tourists do not comprehend that pure white light.
The art professor makes a formal note.
I, but half-ruined, feel the ancient grace,
The terror of the Virgin's face,
The hint, like the fresh herb beside her throat,
Of ever-lost delight.

We clean the varnish, cannot see to clean
Our clogged lies, lusts, treasons, sloths, vanities;
We use the lilies of our sex to know,
And cannot therefore see to know
The vision in whose light the virgin sees,
Nor know what sin might mean.

Nature is made the proxy for our shame;
Pollution is the name we give the grief
Of self-despoiled and ravished innocence.
We make machines do penitence
To the dim spectres of our disbelief,
Absolving us of blame.

The closest we can come is in denial:
Think how the fogs clear from a mountainside
To show the galleries of virgin trees,
When the dawn's dazzling mysteries
Remind us of the soul's lost passiontide,
The sources of its Nile.

In a Season of Political Faction

The slow spring lifts its body once again
As if it were a ship swamped in a gale;
It rights itself. An avalanche of pain
Pours from its battered bows across the rail.
But every time it settles deeper in,
Its shell-like skies and petals overwhelmed:
How can the frail and fragrant jessamine
Contest the governance of a thing unhelmed?
The cold salt in its tons runs everywhere,
And kills whatever is still sweet and warm:
No blossoming of fleshy peach or pear
Can coax an ounce of pity from the storm.
And now the light fades, and the hour grows late:
Over the waste blows the dark wind of hate.

A Riddle

This sickness thirsts, but hates desire,
Chills when it burns, but is not fire;
Sweet-tasting to the fair and just,
But once it catches, sour as dust;
Pretends to free the human race,
Makes monsters of the human face;
Corrupts the meaning of the mother,
Turns he and she against each other;
Twists truth into an ancient lie,
But has no shame to testify;
Servile, despising those who serve,
Seeking what it would not deserve;
Cyst upon the human heart,
Canker of science and of art;
Gives love a new excuse to hate,
Envies the power to create,
And yet can only imitate.

What is it?

On a Bigot of the Poststructuralist Persuasion

How those deformed ideas, noseless, blind,
So deeply root themselves within the mind
And draw the eyes apart and sag the skin
And blur the face as if stretched by a pin,
And make a terrified confusion, where
The noble human glance should clear the air;
And make of childhood a soiled memory
Of innocence deceived by irony,
And turn a moiety of the human race
Into masked cannibals without a face,
The image of that very fear of void
Which gnaws the bowels of the paranoid;
And make of love a haggling of need,
And history a gnashing pit of greed,
And freedom but the power to oppress,
And family a bond of beastliness,
And truth the looted spoils of the cruel,
The beautiful, the most contemptible.

The human face is made to catch the light,
And show the gravest tremble of delight,
The laughter of the world, wisp of sea-foam
That knows this holy universe as home;

Let it not shrivel in this twisted mask,
And let it not be too much that we ask
That we may have the power to love it still,
Even when its dear good is turned to ill.

Advice to a Poet

Then should you tell them what they want to hear?
They want it so badly, they yearn for it,
It would so ease the pain there is in living;
And they have begged you through their intermediaries,
Not rudely, but with a sad, moving tact;
For once be gentle with them, say the words,
Put it on record, give the great permission.

And who are you to be the judge of things?
What vote made you the guardian of their souls?
—A lesser poet in a century
That has got tired of poets, and with reason:
There were so many, and then after all
Turned out no better than the rest of us—
And you bring no solution to the problem,
No innovation in the craft or theme,
Are an apostle of the ancient forms
And only sing the old discarded dream.

For after all if there is no solution,
No fresh alternative to work and love
And clear intelligence and careful knowing,
No better source of wisdom but ourselves,
No secret way to hand on our decisions

To some director, natural or divine,
Perhaps collective — gender, race, or class —
Then life would be unbearable, we'd see
Reflected in the mirror just a face,
The common vector of some six desires.

And moral perfectness feels so like death!
And you who tell them this have no pretension
Of scoring better on that test than they:
You are as sensual, slothful, as dishonest,
As vain of your good judgment as are they:
And even this is one more form of boasting,
Which does not make it any the less true.

But they would so reward you if you said it,
And after all what harm now would it do?
Say it then, make the required confession:
You will feel so much better when you're through.

Salvage

Imagine you have built a house on sand,
and all our houses yet are built on sand:
and the evening comes,
and the night comes,
when the great storm casts the sea against the land;

an island is the tilted living room,
a brief cape is the brine-sopped sleeping room:
leavings of your lives,
all your past lives,
shifted by small currents in the sea's clear womb;

and you had nought to do but let it go,
let go the wardrobe, let the bookshelves go,
plates, cups fall away,
honors fall away,
records void, ink made once again to flow.

And as young lovers in an ancient storm
you walked in lamplight in a dying storm
under blowing leaves,
green-smelling leaves,
and all you had was sweet love to keep you warm;

so now as ancient creatures jewelled with stone,
swift and incalculable, living stone,
you begin again,
the sin again,
tenderly clothing the tempestuous bone.

205 Woodside Drive

This is the house where your children played by the fireplace;
In spring the blooming wisteria scented the air;
Sundays you kissed in bed and fetched the newspaper:
Now you're a stranger there.

Another family brushes the turn of the banister,
Somebody's photographs clutter the baby grand.
You can see from the sidewalk, straining to get the best angle,
As if in a foreign land.

If you were to trespass, and cross the invisible boundary
Dividing the past from the present, you'd end up in jail.
Your freehold is void. A recording angel would indicate
Signatures marking the sale.

Perhaps it's a nightmare you're having; you'll wake in a panic,
And slowly the desolate dream will slacken and wane,
And you'll see the familiar shadows branching the curtains
And turning you'll drowse off again.

But this is no dream; your body is twenty years older,
The children are distant, the furniture carried away;
All you have left is the joy of the folly of falling,
The dream of the everyday;

All you have left is the heart that harrows its memories;
Here's no abiding stay.

The Arrival Matters

Down this white-hot avenue
In a grayish-silver haze,
I am driving under blue
And brilliant centuries of days;

And a south wind blows and blows,
Tosses the crepe-myrtle trees
White and mauve and pink and rose,
Blows the pollen and the bees;

Where the paving-lines converge
In their clot of blazing mist,
Where the sky and city merge,
Is the point where I exist.

On Glenn Gould's Goldberg Variations, Saint-Colombe, Marais, Radnóti and Petrarch

Consider Orpheus, who fearlessly
Walked step by step into the holocaust;
Those fires were nothing to him, who had lost
More than his life in his Eurydice;
It must have been a rare trance in which he
Perceived those roaring ovens that he must
Traverse as but the soft and primrose mist
Hanging at sunrise between grass and tree;
So taken would a mere man have to be
With death and with death's music that his dust
(That is, his flesh) were calm as any ghost,
Pursuing, gently and persistently,
That other ghost whose face he could not see.
Pass on your calm and your despair to me.

Death Mass

1. Elegy for a Cat, Christmas 1990 (Introit)

i.

There's cause enough for weeping on the Earth:
The soldiers' first and only year as men,
Bernstein and Copland dead, this Christmas birth
Of sacrifice again;

And it's the anniversary of him
Whose mind has fathered me as did his body,
Whose death has shorn our wisdom of a limb—
My own outrageous daddy;

As helpless boats borne to the waterfall
And disappear in its tumultuous glow,
They all go on before us, great and small,
Untethered, with the flow;

So it's a luxury to mourn this cat,
This little merry animal of ours,
This graceful clown, this comic acrobat,
Whose absence chills the hours;

But we shall weep for him, rightly or not:
He was a miracle we did not choose,
A gift we did not know that we had got,
And perforce grieve to lose.

ii.

Paint him in thought, his fur of whitish fawn,
His face velvety black, his tail and paws;
His blue and crosseyed stare, amazing yawn,
Ignoring the applause;

This was the only animal I've known
Who had the true mind of the scientist.
Water was all his study: where's he gone,
Catdom's hydrologist?

Ah, we go armored into that good night:
Math is our breastplate, and the logos sings,
A bright sword in our hand; and we can fight
With fame and art, the wings

Of angels, and the glory of the state,
The promises of heaven, and the city
Graved with the names of heroes consecrate:
And so the more the pity

They, whose sole garment and possession is
Their body's agile life, their quick warm breath,
Should thus so naked and alone, like this,
Be cast out into death.

iii.

How slablike was that sodden thing, how cold.
As little was his case, it weighed like lead.
When he was warm no gravity could hold
Him, even playing dead.

Life's like a blazing sphere, an envelope
Blown up against the pressure of the dark.
His witty innocence was like the hope
That wakes us with the lark.

I'll never find him in my bag again,
Or lying in the sink, a mess of fur,
Or when I sit in weariness and pain,
Feel him jump up and purr.

All I can do is send him with this poem,
As Mozart sent his starling with an air
Drawn from its own song, like a chromosome,
Into we know not where.

And Skelton, with the death of Philip Sparrow,
Seeded the line of English poetry,
And things so grand can grow from what's so narrow,
Though he is lost to me.

iv.

Is it an empty myth that Jesus lay
In straw between a dumb ox and an ass?
He is our son, and there will come a day
Strange as the words of Mass,

When angel children, wise with their software,
Will pinch off universes of new time,
And through the darkened tunnel beckon where
We struggle in our slime;

And may they know of Mookie, this good beast,
Among the myriads of more renown,
And count him for a servant, if the least:
Their harlequin and clown.

Envoi

I have a journey shortly for to go.
This emissary sent forth from the ark,
Whose parting set one eastern star to glow,
Must guide me through the dark:

He's my familiar, my crosseyed friend,
Who'll never know the way, which is as well,
For there's no path there, there beyond the end,
But what a clown can spell.

2. At the Modern Language Association (Judica me; Kyrie)

This is the ugliest death: dishonesty.
I would bring down the temple in my rage:
I'm sick enough with our stupidity
To crush the prisoner as break his cage.

Our time has its own scribes and pharisees,
Those whited sepulchres, who must betray
The living word to cruel parentheses,
The endless circles of the M.L.A..

That worse-than-death, that cowardly self-serving,
The sheer exhaustion of so many lies,
The elevation of the undeserving,
The moral fall grotesquely deemed a rise;

Such terror's in political correctness:
Fear of our unoriginality,
Fear of the vision of our own abjectness,
Fear above all that we might cease to be —

Belated fear, of its own origin,
Consciousness peering down into its hole,
Death being only how we know our sin,
The self a ghost above its own dead soul.

Ah, terrible dilemma, that our best,
Most generous, intents be turned to ill.
How noble that we should deny the West
And count as interest our own good will:

But if we make a hero of the Other,
We cannot but make villains of ourselves;
And so our soul is farmed out to our brother,
And all our motive to do good dissolves.

And if our moral purity requires
That we should starve ourselves in heart and soul,
We do but render us to the cold fires
Of lust, greed, power, out of all control.

And then the cruelty of those who've risen
Into those heights where truth is laughed to scorn!
Most cruel to those who share their trap and prison,
Bound by the ghosts of loves that they've outgrown,

But cruel enough, by office and delay,
To chill the life-warmth of the fresh-eyed young,
To wear the poet down, to kill the play,
To dull the generous spirit of the strong.

But this is all to turn the hemorrhage
Of life, whose moments are too thin and fleeting
To bear the freight of paradise, to rage
Against the vampire-victims of its bleeding;

Those discourse-analysts, Foucauldians,
Are nothing but the rot that comes with death;
What broke them is the very thing that bends
Me to my breaking, and makes short my breath,

Till I too wish for death, can barely speak,
My poet's singing cluttered up with dust,
And feel the cowardice of all critique
Etch and eat up my native iron, like rust.

3. The Persimmon Tree (Gloria)

The glowing moment of Matisse and Stevens,
The bright, green wings, pink dancers in the blue,
Those heavenly earths, and those immanent heavens—
Oh how I wish that vision might be true!

But I admit it now: that world has failed
As surely as the Reich and Soviet
—not utterly. A glory still has trailed
More wildly by my steps, more wildly yet

As I grow older, and the vision burns
Behind the blue skies of this Texas plain,
And sometimes on the gold suburban lawns
Fall blessings, torrents of supernal rain;

And always by my wife's warm side at night
I know the perfect stillness of old love;
And there's that cat—a charm and a delight—
And brave Vivaldi wingtipped like a dove;

And walking out one day beside the lake,
I found myself by a persimmon tree
That offered all its fruit for all to take,
And all the meadow smelled of fruit to me,

And like a holy, hushed society,
The birds came up and took what they could bear,
And as a lover sucks what he can see,
I mouthed the sweet globes that were given there ...

Ah, it's so lovely and so dear, this life!
But it's too frail a cable for its watts:
Think how Van Gogh set by his painter's knife
There in the cornfield, and blew out his guts.

That gentle, charming cat—now I remember:
It comes on me like shade upon the heart—
Was throttled by a mad dog this December,
And that small grief defeated all my art.

When I was young I thought life all the sweeter
That death was waiting to cut off my time;
Death was the mother of beauty, the meter
That gave a line a shape with its end-rhyme.

And in my innocence and self-concern
I scarcely mourned the dead, was not bereaved;
Then later, when a dearer one must burn,
I felt a strange rejoicing as I grieved;

Now, though my own death's but a holiday
That I look forward to, but would not haste,
The deaths of others are unbearable, they weigh
Me down, the dark, the dear loss, and the waste.

And now I feel a fury at the moment
That will not hold for long enough to feel
The lovely complex of its full bestowment,
The secret intricacy of the real.

4. Mene, Mene, Tekel, Upharsin (Dies irae)

How strange, to be thus interrupted by
The war—the very canto broken off,
The logic of the argument awry,
The era past before it said enough.

And even now the bombs are falling on
The scared and ignorant armies of Iraq,
And a new beast-King kneels in Babylon
As words of fire are written on his dark;

And it is we who weigh him, find him wanting,
Our finger writes and having writ moves on;
Our fiery or our cloudy pillar pointing
Across the desert where the great star shone;

And so we have gone back to where it started,
To what was old when Abraham was young,
And we, the youngest and most simple-hearted,
Carry the dreadful burden of the song;

Our boyish pilots bred in Alabama,
Our capable black grunts in camouflage,
Our lean girl-soldiers, reenact the drama
Of holy justice, real or mirage;

And if it is illusion, it is one
That they would die for, in their own brusque fashion;
And what is real, if it's not the sun
Shining upon the morning of their passion?

Better to die for oil (though that's not it),
Than live to only live, and live, and live,
A want-machine for making sex and shit —
Die even for an abstract substantive.

The only sweetness is in sacrifice.
We only have that which we give away.
The *for* -ness of a life gives all the grace
That makes the difference of flesh and clay.

But this is just the creed of the jihad!
The cruellest, most hardened terrorist
Surely must shiver with the breath of God,
And when he smells upon the morning mist

Of some exotic airfield the cold fume
Of kerosene, his hair stands up on end
With life electrified with martyrdom:
We cannot trust our yearning to transcend.

5. *The Ghosts (Confutatis maledictis)*

All day I have been ridden by a ghost:
I think, the spirit of Michel Foucault.
He's in such agony, hating and lost,
Like the oiled seabirds in the the undertow

That pulls along the Saudi littoral,
Where now another acolyte of Power
Oozes the sumps of the political
Into the blue petals of the worldflower;

58

I see his knees and elbows skinned and raw,
He hugs them to himself, his bulging eyes
Stare to and fro, a frightened minotaur,
His buttocks like a running cicatrice;

The huge sarcoma-blotches on his skin
Display the final phase of that disease
Which is the body's death of discipline,
Decision not to punish, but appease;

Its great refusal to define the Other
As other than itself, its hate for fixity —
And all I feel is pain for this my brother,
A ghastly leaden grief, a sickened pity.

And what is terrible about this shade
Is that he's from the future, not the past.
For now it comes to me, the hell he made
Is one of many shadows that are cast

Like branches into all the time to come,
And has its own reality, and sends
This phantom into my delirium
To kill all voices that frustrate its ends;

And thus in this poor ghost a whole world screams
That it may have some space to gnaw its being;
And seeks to colonize my thoughts and dreams,
And set its spies within my very seeing.

But who is there to exorcise this thing,
This knot of nausea behind my shoulder,
Who will release my voice that aches to sing
Of beauty that survives its own beholder?

And here the poem broke; but now today
Another ghost, dearest of my dead friends,
My sweet and foul-mouthed Mozart, came to stay,
And get a birthday-present at my hands;

And any future blessed and led by him
Cannot be absolutely dark and cold;
He wrote the music which the cherubim
Shall play, newborn, on their kazoos of gold.

And even if there is another present,
Realer and richer, like a shell of blue,
Where Mozart did not die, but convalescent
Wrote his *Geist-Insel*, lived to eighty-two,

And everybody laughed at Robespierre,
And Holocausts and Gulags were unknown,
But Vernean cosmonauts, upon a dare,
In 1920 landed on the Moon—

Yet even so, our branch of time is fed,
My darling Amadeus, with your blood;
And still puts out, despite the evil dead,
The white and dazzling flowers of the good.

6. *The Parting Beyond the End of Time (Lesson: 1 Cor. 15)*

Imagine with me, if you will, a stage.
Two striking people enter, man and wife;
She's loved him since the start of middle age,
And he has loved her all his adult life.

The play is set some forty-five years hence.
They could be you or I, though "well-preserved":
They're quick, judgmental, with the elegance
That comes with great achievements well-deserved.

They have but newly come from some award;
He's loosened his bow-tie, like Spencer Tracy;
She's kicked off one black shoe, and he has poured
Two glasses of white wine, befoamed and lacy.

They live in France. Their children variously
Devote their lives to human benefit:
Art, science, law, music and charity.
They quarrel and make up with love and wit.

And it appears that drugs and medicines
Can now prolong a life; eternal youth,
The long quest of the Taoist mandarins,
Is now no cloudy dragon, but a truth.

And so already, though she's ninety-eight,
She starts to show the flush of a past age;
Soon she'll begin again to menstruate,
Her book flipped back to an unwritten page.

She feels that lovely female alchemy
Which opens up the world's unruly springs;
Forgets the first-laid layers of memory,
Remembers, as the old do not, new things.

But he, though hale and vigorous, refuses
The measures that deceive the deathbound cell;
And day by day it seems the years she loses
Are added to his own, as by a spell.

And so their little party turns to grief;
They see each other, cannot speak for tears;
He makes a little joke for the relief,
How he had only signed for seventy years;

And she breaks out in anger, that he'd leave,
That he was tired of her, that he'd prefer
Death for his mistress, that he would deceive
His lover with an inexpensive whore.

And he goes on so patiently that he
Has written out his life like an old play,
That it's act five, with nothing left to be,
And nothing in act six for him to say.

"I fired my life in this trajectory,
And if it misses, all I am is waste;
By dying I protect your stake in me,
Preserving what you valued undisgraced;

"For if I were a young immortal fellow,
Might not the years we had seem like a dream?
And might I not get weary of one pillow,
And find our memories an outworn game?

"For me that would be kiting on a check.
I'll cash it out for you when I will die.
I am an old fool on my quarterdeck,
But when my ship goes down then so will I."

"Then I must die with you, like pharaoh's wife?"
"That isn't what I mean. You've made your choice.
For you the great work is unending life,
How to make meaning of it, make a voice

"To sing forever out of deathlessness,
And make a death of shadows and of loss,
Of parting and of time's forgetfulness —
To make a gravity from weightless mass."

But this is not the ending of our play.
Suppose there is a life after our death.
Imagine now that on that dreadful day,
He finds, as in a dream, he can take breath

After the drowning fall into the deep.
Would not this gentle parting from his wife
Into what he had thought might be a sleep
Be worse than any grief of death or life?

7. Murders (Confiteor)

But does it matter if we die tomorrow
Or live a thousand years, if life's a drug
That dims and muffles its own joy and sorrow,
And wears its innocence down to a shrug?

But why blame life? The plants and animals
Feel every pain and pleasure in their skins;
Rocks, clouds, and stars are all originals:
If I am drugged, then it is by my sins.

This is the subject that I could not touch:
Not only my vulgarities of lust,
Not only the dishonesties, and such
Grey money-dealings as are masked in trust,

Those hideous shadows that eat up my light,
That bloat my simple Fredness with disease,
And waste my parents' love for me, and spite
The promise of my gifts—not only these,

But huge unpunishable crimes that kill
The soul—one that I cannot speak at all,
And three that were the children of my will
If, in the world's law, nothing criminal.

I slew three fathers and I kept the gains.
One was a foolish and great-hearted man,
Who was my senior, and who mocked my brains,
But sought me as a friend and partisan.

64

I had a project, and he thwarted me,
As retrograde to his intent and plan;
And by success and cold hostility
I broke the great heart of that foolish man.

Indeed he should not pit his brittle horn
Against a young stag hardened in the snows;
He lent an axe that I did not return,
And bled his life out through his ruptured nose.

Years later I returned where we'd contend.
I met his son, a fine young man, but slow;
He greeted me with trust, his father's friend;
I knew then what a murderer must know.

And then there was the poet, whose good word
Had opened doors for me I would not break;
Who when I was an editor, inferred
That I might publish him for old time's sake;

And when I did not, then the big old man
Came to my party and began to shout;
I felt the wrath of the Promethean,
And took him by the coat and threw him out.

And for his poems, some had honesty;
And for his insults, some were justified;
For me he was the damned majority;
I heard a few months later he had died.

And then there was the time my father told
Of how he loved two women, not just one;
My snow-white lilies, with their throats of gold
Stood round us in the mild spring afternoon;

My mother knew him and would share his life,
But being what I am, I would not yield;
My honor, born of his, became the knife
That dealt the wound that never can be healed.

The cruelty we do, we do not know:
He was the unicorn, one of a kind;
I did not see Death at his saddle-bow;
For he renounced that love, and I was blind;

And on his deathbed, with his smitten heart,
He begged me to protect her like my own:
And shortly after, she for her own part
Fell sick and died, in terror and alone;

And I inherited from him his name;
I use his gift, a box of good steel tools;
Perhaps I even stole some of his fame,
Wisest and most unquestioning of fools:

Ah, terribly, they trust me, though it seems
I come as death in my dark innocence;
I feel no guilt; I do not have bad dreams;
This is no easy case of penitence.

And yet these sins become a screen, a wall,
That bars me from that deeper seeing-twice
Of lovely, fading, mortal life, and all
The tint and sweet of daily paradise.

8. *Metaphysics (Sanctus)*

The anecdote of self is but a chatter,
A voice that will not cease, but in our sleep;
And when the morning comes, it makes a clatter,
And starts again, a flock of panicked sheep;

And this is what our science, or our savior
Would rescue for a hundred million years?
A trillion selves trapped in their own behavior,
Insane, on shrieking edge, and bored to tears?

We could not bear our immortality
Unless some deepening were moulded in,
Some infinite digression were to be
Thrust into every moment unforeseen;

But this were so already, if we knew
This very world in all its dear decaying;
I am an animal, a bird that flew
Into a concert-hall where Mozart's playing,

And cannot understand a single note:
Had I but ears to hear, the twist of time
Were loosened like a collar from my throat,
And I would learn to sing the requiem.

So we must be enlarged and iterated,
Our bandwidth must be broadened, and our sense
Must be slowed down to realtime, and mated
With software of divine intelligence.

Suppose that there's a progress in the good,
A rustling of angels in the wings,
And time will bring about a brotherhood
And sisterhood of new awakenings;

Suppose our honest science should achieve
The ancient purposes of alchemy:
Not the mere gold of everlasting life
But metamorphosis and setting-free,

And the brain crawled from its dim chrysalis,
And the soul tutored in its lexicon,
And planets wakened into genesis,
And sweet new children born in silicon,

And bodies taught to sing in every cell,
And jacked into the secret life of things,
And, Solomonic, able now to tell
The animals' and plants' imaginings;

Then might not such a city of descendants
Seek back into its blinded ancestry,
And pity us from its amazed transcendence,
And by its very knowing, make us be;

Just as the universe itself, they say,
Chose from all origins there could have been
The one that led to such rich time and play
That it would by its fruits be known and seen;

And so it is a strange and holy thing
To labor in the world and love its goals,
Even, intent upon its bettering,
Postpone the purifying of our souls.

The causes of the world no longer run
From past to future only, but turn back
And bless the places where they have begun,
And turn again upon their former track,

And deepen every time, and add detail,
Until the finer focusings reveal
Innermore branchings, scale nested in scale,
The infinite attractor of the real.

Then what if, with their magic scholarship,
Our branched descendants should have found the art
To reconstruct, down to each fingertip,
The bodies of the dead, our mind and heart?

We dying, then, look back upon our flesh
With the incipient eyes of resurrection;
When we grope down the cave, feeling the fresh
Light pouring through, the dawnlight of perfection,

And see the kindly ones stand waiting there,
(Perhaps a father or a mourned-for wife),
Are not those angels on their golden stair
The very fruits of how we lived our life?

And is not one of them, we cannot see
Because the light beyond makes such a glow,
Our own self, but enabled and set free,
To ask the question if we'd stay or go?

Perhaps the shallowness of what we do
Denotes it as an early iteration;
We only feel a random déjà vu,
A faint, angelical anticipation;

Perhaps the deepening of the attractor
Will bring us round again to where we were,
And then the limitation of the actor
Will fold itself in music to a sphere,

And every blazing sphere will be a fruit
Fed by the branches of the tree of time,
All paradises from a single root,
All variations on a paradigm ...

But these abstractions are the very sign
The broth of time is thin and dissolute:
It must be thickened up with heat and wine,
As music deepens in *The Magic Flute.*

The heat is tragedy, the wine is death.
Our being is a metempsychosis.
Ah, angel children, gotten on our breath,
Lend us the wakening terror of your kiss.

9. Undoing (Lux aeterna)

i.

I had intended to complete the nine
With some renunciation of thought things,
A casting-off the self that I call mine,
A last unpinioning of this the poet's wings,

And in that silence, to have heard the sea,
And in that darkness, to have seen the light
Of all the denseness of reality.
Alas, things did not go as I had hoped they might.

For having cast three demons from my mind,
Opinion, self, and poetry, behold
A worse one entered in, a double-bind
That by my weakness multiplied a thousandfold.

The self that cast out self was now quite bare;
It stung with petty grievances and spite;
It was a coward, and it feared the air,
And, in a swift despair, it sinned against the light.

And yet another death had been revealed,
An endless maze I wandered in the murk.
I prayed then to the muses, to be healed,
And heard a chuckle, and was told "go back to work."

                ii.

That laugh contained the sting of a reproach:
Not the stern father to the erring son,
But as a brave lieutenant might approach
A loved old general about to turn and run.

And even now we pause in our campaign,
Knowing too sharply that we may be wrong,
And like Arjuna feel the endless pain
Of all the innocents we kill to make the song;

But if our children are the gods, then we
Cannot curl up in their ungotten womb,
Must put on the absurd authority
That sets a parent's soul at hazard to assume;

And if the world is far too interwoven
For us to justly act in it at all,
Yet action is the feedback of the given
From which the patterned world emerges in its fall.

Who wrought the murder of the innocents?
Herod, who sent his blood-drenched soldiery?
The bearers of the gold and frankincense?
Or the bright child they sought on that epiphany?

iii.

As those who, dying, recapitulate
In a swift fugue of moments all they've been,
This ninth cadenza sums the other eight
As if by closure to find out what they might mean.

The first meant unrecuperable grief;
The second meant the living death of lies;
The third told how it could not be enough
To live till death a life of only ears and eyes;

The fourth spoke of the glory of the wars
That cannot canonize their sacrifice;
And in the fifth two ghostly visitors
Pleaded their causes, power against gentle grace;

The sixth was a play-parable, wherein
Were told the traps of immortality;
The seventh confessed the killing power of sin;
The eighth, the comforts of a new philosophy.

Now in the ninth, what trope will serve to bind
The last lines to the first, what magic rhyme
Will leap like laserlight from mind to mind,
And close the involuting circuitry of time?

iv.

Let it be nothing but the blue, blue sky.
I saw it lately, like a bowl of light,
Unmarred by any purchase to the eye,
So pure it offered nothing that might catch the sight.

And yet a thousand colors trembled there,
Depth below depth, iris and amethyst,
Sapphire and periwinkle films of air,
Absence and presence that could strangely coexist;

I saw that shining roundness as a breast
Whose offered nipple was the darkbright sun,
As mother first and lover at the last—
And knew that "heaven" was neither metaphor nor pun.

The warm wind made me tremble, and I knew
The white annunciation of the spring;
A green as brilliant as was the blue
Glowed in the fields, the earth's awakening.

But still there was a meaning in the skies
I could not catch, and now it comes to me:
I saw that blue last in my poor cat's eyes,
And cannot help but laugh at the absurdity.

I break off one more time and go outside.
The moon is new, a presage of new wars.
It is quite dark. The blown clouds cannot hide
The blueblack sky strewn with its plenitude of stars.

North Sea Storm

Zuidzande, Zeeland, August 1993
For Marleen van Cauwelaert

The wind that blows across the polders blows
The end of one age, the birth of another.
Turn of the century weather.
It blusters by the eaves and throws
A scarred branch at the chimney-stack
Over and over.
We hear it in the attic bedroom, twitch and crack,
Secret, invisible, speaking of the sea.
The mourning doves take shelter in the lee.
Over and over they repeat the track:

It's too true, Tookturoo,
It's too true, Tookturoo.
My friends and I are plotting the next century.
The wind that blows across the polders blows
A branch of ripened pears across the sky;
Hesitates, rises, swings across and falls.
The overloaded apple-tree
Can only jerk and shake.
In all this dreadful pother
Something must surely fall and die;
Something must surely come to be.
The storm is whining at the walls.
The grasses on the dyke are all bowed one way.
The little orchard glows
With green, with green beneath the cold grey sky.
It's too true, Tookturoo.
Something is stretching itself awake.
The wind that blows the northern sea
Will blow us all away.
The wind that blows across the polders blows
Day into night, night into day.
It's too true, Tookturoo.
It's too true, Tookturoo.

On Robert Corrigan

When he was young the world-street was his stage.
A big red Irishman in New Orleans,
He lived the lover's and the fighter's age
And the set rattled when he played his scenes.

And then, the great director, he would move
Among the myths and dragons of the time;
He made Monroe and Gable fall in love,
The decades danced in his dark pantomime;

And then he took the audience by its ears,
And like a string of apple-trees, he sowed
New schools to teach new laughter and new tears;

And then at last became the very stage
We act and walk on, he became the road,
The world, the setting of our pilgrimage.

Corrigan Dying

Now as I write within this house in Zeeland
Corrigan's dying in his bed in Texas.
They say he cannot eat or speak; they say
Not one but many illnesses consume him.
They say his big old body's wasted all away.
He is my friend, my liege, my old campaigner.
O lords of time, grant good speed to my plane
That I may come in time to say goodbye.

Corrigan Dead

Last week I saw him, and he gaped and slept.
He seemed to me a deadly sick old man,
But still belonged to this side, with the living.
I took his hand, and spoke to him, and wept,
Took those small liberties that well we can
With those who're done with taking and with giving.

This week I left him just before he died.
He'd changed, I hardly recognized his face.
His great nose stood out nobly, like a knight.
He now belonged upon the other side.
I wondered if he dreamed; his ghastly grace
Made him a mottled essence carved of light.

Now he is dead, though, I feel all his life
Released about us in its golden flood.
Mad Corrigan still rides the harvest moon!
How strange, I hear his chuckle in the grief;
The clear Fall weather has his brilliant mood,
Mocking us gently this bright afternoon.

Field Notes

It has begun. For forty nights and days
I fought the coming of the holy ghost.
- / - / - / - / - /
I fasted and I prayed.

How can I say what's in my heart to say?

I am a sad shepherd.

My thoughts pass through me as swiftly as the great
cloud shadows that pass over Judea.

I see them from this last ledge before the blind waste of
Arabia Deserta.

I have stood, a virgin, up to my thighs in the Jordan.

The river Jordan is chilly and cold

Chills the body but not the soul

I have lived, like the wild man John, on locusts and wild
    honey.
The ravens have dropped manna beside me as I lay.
I have drunk the clear water that oozes from the rock of
    the haggadah.
I have been drunk for days upon starvation, upon the
    turning of the sun shadows, upon the turning of the
    stars,

Upon the terrible speed of my own thoughts,

Upon pity for the sheep under my care,

Upon the unmeasurable depth of every moment, its iteration
through the beginning of time, its iteration through the last
moments when the stars all died, and out of the wreck of time
the Holy Ghost brought forth the very universe which was
now ending, and thus the snake of days turned back upon its
beginning, and seized its own tail — whose venom was the medi-
cine, the pharmakon for the sickness of its ending, the sweet
oil of a new life, the mystical elixir of eternal renewal.

I was in the courts of heaven praised as a poet, though I am
but an indifferent maker beside many who have counted me
their god. As a fashioner of parables I did well. But for the

purpose of these notes all my art has forsaken me.

I had devised a form of verses for these scholia, these field-notes that you have asked me to record, for this science is one that will ask all the depth of poetry. But I cannot hold the form. It was to follow the shape of the looped cross, akin to the ankh of the Egyptians, but with the head of the cross produced, and looped over to become its horizontal member. I draw it in the dust, so:

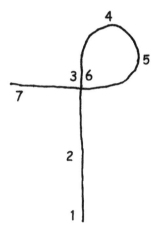

The first line, of five metrical feet, was to represent the foot of the cross. The second, of like length, would mark the point half-way from the foot to the crossing, so as to indicate the relative length of the vertical member. The third, likewise of five feet, should mark the crossing itself. The fourth would mark the highest altitude of the cross, but because it merely grazed that measure, and did not cross it, would contain three feet only. This line would rhyme with the first, in token of the echo or match between the topmost and the bottommost part of any sensible object. The fifth line would mark the furthest lateral extent of the loop to the right, and again would be penalized in length because of its tangential nature, containing but four feet, and rhyming with the second line. The sixth line in the verse would again mark the crossing, but in the horizontal, not the vertical dimension. It would repeat the entire third line, as was appropriate, since it would occupy the same position in the figure. The last line would represent the ending and completion of the figure, and its furthest lateral extent to the left side. It would be of five metrical feet, and rhyme with the first and fourth lines. Thirty-two feet would be in the completed measure, that is two to the power five, or 100,000 in the binary notation.

The whole verse, and the figure of which it was the melodic enumeration, should represent the actual shape of time at any moment: that is, at the crossing of the loop, which was the present, there should be two currents of causation: a strong determinative and direct one from the past below, what Aristotle called the material and accidental, and a weak persuasive and indirect one from the future above, what Aristotle called the formal and final. And the result should be a new and open vector, at right angles to the direction of time, standing for what the religious call eternity.

This was the form I had devised; but my head has been so dizzy with the fumes of the desert that my craft has left me and I am able only to repeat the maze through which I reasoned out the form. Let us try again.

Field Notes

1. The Temptation in the Desert

It has begun. For forty nights and days
I fought the coming of the holy ghost.
The small rains fell upon the desert sand.
I wandered in a maze
Of gullied washouts. I was lost.
The small rains fell upon the desert sand.
I fasted and I sang the psalms of praise.

For still this desert is the promised land.
What words to choose, how may it be revealed
To You, Who have healed up the wounded world,
How tender to the hand
Is every lily of the field? —
To You, Who have healed up the wounded world,
What riches grow out of this worn-out sand?

Here for ten thousand years were kings
Who built their tels and hunted droves of deer.
Men came from the Euphrates and cut trees.
Goats ate all living things.
The spring rains faltered year by year.
Men came from the Euphrates and cut trees,
And yet it's sweeter for its ravishings.

My body—sewn with invisible software
So that my head is haloed with its waves—
My body has grown smoky with the fasts,
Privation has made dear
Its caskets, gates and cabled naves.
My body has grown smoky with the fasts:
I could forget the taste of heaven here.

What sweeter to a space-time traveller
Than be a carpenter in Nazareth?
From a stone cup at dawn I drank goat's milk,
At noon I sweated myrrh,
At evening felt the ocean's breath,
From a stone cup at dawn I drank goat's milk,
And Mary kissed and gathered me to her.

Upon that glittering night of my first Mass
When I rose from the warm womb of my mother
And felt the cold breeze with its blazing star,
The great ox and the ass
Breathed honey on me as their brother
And felt the cold breeze with its blazing star
And saw, though bestial, the angels pass.

Ten billion years had prepared for this.
The dark gave birth to light, the light divided,
Condensed into the stars, and came to life;
And out of the abyss,
Self-knowing soul, the spirit glided,
Condensed into the stars, and came to life,
Returning at the end to genesis.

In the meantime I had a life to live.
I smelt the woodsmoke, tasted Tyrian wine;
I broke the unleavened bread of Passover.
I was a fugitive,
Forgot to serve the great design,
Broke the unleavened bread of Passover,
Buried myself in pastoral narrative.

And You permitted this, as You permit
This weak and faltering journal of a man,
Though for each breaking of the laws of time
Galaxies go unlit,
Worlds die before their lives began;
Though at each breaking of the laws of time
The denseness of the real must pay for it.

The public record of my life must be
Of certainty, of love, of sacrifice.
Here only I record my doubts, my pleasures,
Backstage anxiety,
The mental games of living twice,
Here only I record my doubts, my pleasures,
An anthropologist in Arcady.

Still I have wished that time would never cease,
Held by the Virgin in her lovely arms,
Suckled in fumes of frankincense and gold;
I was the prince of peace,
The goat-boy of the sleeping farms

Suckled in fumes of frankincense and gold,
The lilies' fragrance and the shepherd's fleece;

But all the time could not forget the cost
Herod exacted from the innocents;
How I was bought, and shall be bought, by death,
And gentle futures lost,
How ghosts haunt every providence,
How I was bought, and shall be bought, by death,
How I must pay unto the uttermost.

I must go on, out into history.
From John I learned the treachery of fears.
He is so young, so mortal, and so sure,
How can he see to be,
I blinded with my thousand years?
He is so young, so mortal, and so sure,
And even now denying Salome.

It was Your message to me, was it not,
White dove hanging above John's water-shell,
To tell me it is time the planted spy
Must start the fatal plot?
(I must endure my time in hell)
—To tell me it is time the planted spy
Must pay for all the time that he has bought.

The Jordan water flowed across my thighs;
I was to do what always must be done;

It was the same before, when You, my King,
Struck the scales from my eyes,
Named me Your father and Your son,
It was the same before, when You, my King,
Called me to be the beast of sacrifice.

So, it is written that I now must meet
That gentleman, the prince of all the world.

And this is the thing I never made clear, though I tried in every way I could, because the people would never believe it, it was so simple; or they did not want to believe it, couldn't bear to believe it. My brother Gautama always put it better than I; but in India you cannot resist the flood, and he had behind him all the whispers of the Upanishads. My teachers, the sociologists, would say that India understood him because the Brahmins had triumphed over the Kshatriyas; my teachers spoke of the military barrier of the Himalayas, and of the martial art of passive resistance. And yet gentle India waded blood for a hundred years after the British left. Or will wade blood, in that same future I have come to bring about. That all the other futures were—are to be—worse yet I would not believe if I had not seen our studies of them.

But bloodshed and war are not the greatest evil. When I bade them turn the other cheek, some of the best of my followers believed that it was war against which I preached, and took violence to be the gravest of all ills. But the prince of this world is not a soldier, and does not observe the honor of soldiers. A soldier knows the humility of obedience, and the humility of being obeyed. The Gospels tell of my friendship with the centurions, and it will be he who will draw a sword and cut off the ear of Caiaphas' servant, my poor hot-blooded Simon Peter, into whose hands I will give the temporal rule of the church. I come not to bring peace, but a sword.

Who is the prince of this world? Not war. He is power. Not power as we speak of the power of the imagination, or the power of water or of atomic nuclei to drive a mill or turbine, or the power of emotion, or the power of fanaticism, or the power even of greed. He is political power, the cruelty that emanates from the many, when almost any one of the many might repine of it, but a power that nevertheless condenses itself in one leader, the cruelest and most ashamed and most miserable of them all; the pleasure of that one in doing only what the many have silently begged be done; the refreshing certainty of the future purified of all but the foreseen results of the will's intentions, the satisfaction in being the sole cause, or worse, subsuming oneself into the force that is the sole cause—this is the prince of the world.

And this is why I fear the coming of the prince, even when I know how I shall answer him: *not by bread alone doth a man live; he hath given his angels charge over thee; thou shalt not tempt the lord thy god; thou shalt love the lord thy god above all.* I am afraid of being condemned out of my own mouth. For does not a poet— as I am—seek to make a verse that is purified of all but his own intention? Does not an actor—as I am—seek an act of power that will transform possibility into actuality, and make a monopoly of his audience's attention? And does not a holy servant of god seek to subsume himself into the divine will? What makes the difference?

Gift. We only have that which we give away. I must die. And I must learn to pity Satan, who prepares, ten thousand years from now, the subtle argument that will, in his time, have caused me to betray my own time and usher in the events that will lead to his.

So, it is written that I now must meet
That gentleman, the prince of all the world.
His name is legion; he is the regime
Of power made complete,
Knowledge perfected and unfurled.
His name is legion; he is the regime
Whose head consumes the body to its feet.

He is the knowledge that's desire's disguise:
The very death and opposite of science;
Within his belly shriek the souls of those
Who thought his counsel wise,
The world a play of difference;
Within his belly shriek the souls of those
Who took truth, beauty, goodness to be lies.

All I can do is give to him that takes
My body, let him maul it in his jaws;

Its light, immortal poison to a being
Who neither loves nor makes,
Whose envy turns all gift to cause;
Its light, immortal poison to a being
Whose thirst no blood, no gift, no mercy slakes.

I see the whirlwind gather on the plain;
The forces of his cruel futurity
Tearing the naive gases of the air;
He, in his black soutane,
Uniform of the pharisee,
Tearing the naive gases of the air,
Speaks, in his academic voice, to me.

2. *The Transfiguration*

Who, therefore, do the people say I am?
Some say I am Elias, some say John.
How can I tell the truth in Galilee?
Draw them a diagram?
Show logic etched in silicon?
How can I tell the truth in Galilee
Yet keep it to the tongue of Abraham?

I cannot say how time is branched, and flowers
In futures that are fed by what you do,
How each time turns upon itself, and seeks,
Burning its vital powers,

That past most apt to make it true,
How each time turns upon itself, and seeks
To wind back up its own essential clue;

How all of nature branches and augments,
From the first particles to the brain's branched cells;
And how the whorled attractors coax and draw
Their own embodiments
Into the forms of flowers and shells —
And how the whorled attractors coax and draw
The birthing universe to sound and sense.

All I can do is write upon the sand.
A sower cast his seed upon the ground.
The Kingdom's like unto a mustardseed.
The world's end is at hand.
The lost sheep shall indeed be found.
The Kingdom's like unto a mustardseed.
Work, pray, to bring about the promised land.

But then all time is but a parable,
A story told whose meaning slowly grows
Until its end transfigures its beginning,
Making it beautiful;
The bud known truly in the rose,
Until its end transfigures its beginning
And merest matter turns to miracle.

And who am I? I am the son of man.
I am their child, the star of Bethlehem.
When You, the Alpha in the Omega,
Revealed to me Your plan,
You were as far as I to them;
When You, the Alpha in the Omega,
Called me, I was a mere tragedian.

You offered me the greatest role of all,
To play, and be, the incarnated god;
To suffer on the cross, and die, and rise,
King of the carnival;
To shed my consecrated blood,
To suffer on the cross, and die, and rise,
And take the long-awaited curtain-call.

I played my part, then, in Capernaum;
As Dionysos, I turned water into wine;
Tipsy, rode back from Cana by the lake,
With zither, pipe, and drum,
Flowers on the asses' ears, and mine,
Tipsy, rode back from Cana by the lake,
Pink mountains still reflected in its gloom.

The air was liquid as if, deep within the Rift
Where Africa and Asia start to cleave,
The ghost of a great ocean bathed the shore,
As if its slow, sweet drift
Granted to us, who dwelt beneath

The ghost of that great sea that bathed the shore,
Reprieve and refuge, as an unasked gift.

The feasts and rooftops of Capernaum!
The woodfires in the damp and chilly Fall!
Incense and synagogues, Peter and James,
Divine delirium
Of agape and bacchanal,
Incense and synagogues, Peter and James,
Mary and John, the soft symposium.

But they are all so young, and poor, and ill,
And ignorant, these simple fishermen.
Even the strongest is so dim and dying,
A tiny fire of will,
Jude, Thomas, and the Magdalen,
Even the strongest are so dim and dying,
Pity would kill me, had it power to kill.

Oh, it's easy enough to heal the sick and give sight and hearing
back to the blind and deaf. I scarcely need to direct the diag-
nostic and medical software in my brain to make the
submolecular adjustments. A simple word will do it, when the
great aura of love is about us, and the euphoria of the apoca-
lypse gives everything a fine, hysterical edge. Since I know
that they will be healed, whether by the catastrophic changes
in their nervous, endocrine and immune systems that are trig-
gered by divine faith, or by my own little devices, my certainty
is overwhelming. I grieve for the injustice of my power over

them; I could inflict the most horrible cruelties upon them, and they would love me. Indeed, I shall inflict them: the temple razed, the diaspora, the pogroms, the distant burning.

But what will they do with their renewed health, or sight, or hearing, or power of movement? There is a moment of joy at the change; then the usual politics of life, the usual daily inadequacy of feeling, the failure of insight, the blank plodding through the dull moods, the accidia at the height of good fortune, the unrecognized blessings. We in the fortieth century can resurrect them, body and soul, with some expense of timestuff. We can make them immortal, healthy, athletic, cheerful in mood, sexually well-adjusted, and give them a reasonable smile. But for what purpose? Their faces, in this first-century Palestine, are grooved with grief, superstition, passion, paranoia, love, and insane spiritual dedications; they are like their portraits in the old Byzantine churches, their cheeks gaunt, their bald heads domed, their eyes blazing. They are beautiful. In the late twentieth century, when we saw for the first time that health and longevity produced only suburbanites, we sought real experience in the ethnic wars—blue winter skies in the old landscapes smudged with the inferno of burning shopping-malls, hordes of refugees, dead babies in their mothers' arms. Were we so wrong?

Would it be worth bringing all the dead back to life, only to turn them into bored democrats? What would they do to occupy themselves for so many thousand years? Have divorces? Certainly they could not have children, lest, being immortal, they clog the entire universe with human flesh. In the Kingdom there will be neither marrying nor giving in marriage. We must discover a new way of being—in which human soul is rewritten back into the fabric of time and the universe, so as to thicken and deepen it rather than consume it and stretch it thin. But this reinscription is a kind of memory, a memorializing that is infinitely painful and tragic, and in which a mysterious joy arises from the design, in a shriek that is hard to tell from agony. Although the work will need the most subtle technical mastery and material science, it will also take acts of sacrifice and dramas of moral invention.

I come not to bring peace, but a sword. And the meaning of this is that I am the greatest criminal in history. My gospel of love is an engine that will drive unrelenting technical progress, and open so great a gap between the weak and the strong that tens of millions will die in blank, unreasoning pain. I will push Cortez and Pizarro across the oceans with the guns, their horses, and their diseases; and whole civilizations will twist as they burn. Perhaps, as Krishna says, they were all devoted to death already; or as my divine Shakespeare says, "What is't to leave betimes?" This does not, however, make it any easier to kill everything that I have ever cared for.

I preach that they should feed the hungry and clothe the naked; but my words are more for the benefit of the benefactors than of the poor. It is harder for a rich man to enter the Kingdom of Heaven than for a camel to pass through the eye of a needle; but that is not because the rich man is evil, but because he is unhappy, or perhaps even because his happiness is moderate and sane and long-lasting, and this condition breeds despair.

The Father, Who stepped back from His unimaginable time to mine, and instructed me upon my mission, has left it to me to discover the answers. Indeed, His existence, His future, I suspect, depends on this research. He will need its results for His last great struggle to coax the universe retroactively into its beginning. But if with this enterprise we burn up too much of the physical curvature of things, He will not have the resources for His work; or at least the fabric of time and experience which He will set weaving will be shallow and thin, like the half-life of a virtual particle.

I come, I think, to deepen and clear the gates of some inner iteration of attention, some unbearably complicated drama, that I must call simply love.

A week ago I fed five thousand people on five barley loaves and two fishes; I had been talking to them, and at once I felt how hungry they were, how it was after noon and some of them were faint in the sun. It was a crude lapse, I suppose, and very expensive; quasars will be quenched in the time from which I come to pay for it. And even if I had not done it, they would write afterwards that I had done some such thing. I was being fractious in wishing to make their miracles come true. But I don't repent of the conjuring trick—though it was exactly the kind of thing that Satan had suggested in the desert.

If we could mass-produce and iterate meaning, so that one human being might eat five thousand times the life—so that time would be thickened to be five thousand times as precious—so that the appetite for it might be an addiction as mad as teen-age desire, as mad as an old woman's fear of death—and then turned outwards, toward the lovely community of the world—that might be love indeed.

But now I must make my report and justify my expenses to the Lord. I shall let Simon Peter and James and John come too, and I shall speak in Aramaic. According to the scriptures they will think I am speaking with Elias—a mistake they will make again when I am on the cross—but it is Eloi to Whom I shall address myself. We will climb Mount Tabor. They will see me transfigured, in white garments, whiter than any fuller on earth could make them, and my face will shine like the sun.

3. Gethsemane

The city lies before me in the gloam.
The Temple, huge, Mesopotamian,
Broods in its precincts like a golden curse,
Flanked by the hippodrome,
The theatre, the works of man—
Broods in its precincts like a golden curse
Surrounded by the forts and laws of Rome.

The Khedron brook is full this time of year.
I hear it chuckling with a nightingale.

The smell of olives and crushed rosemary
Rises around us here:
Sacrifice-smoke across the vale,
The smell of olives and crushed rosemary,
The city's stink and cooking. Atmosphere.

I am a tourist in this ancient land.
Let this cup pass from me; I am not worth
The task I must perform. To be an actor
—All at second-hand—
Is to be banished from the earth.
The task I must perform's to be an actor
And make spontaneous what is self-command.

When Lazarus my friend was sick, they came
And begged me to his bed that I might heal;
I waited, preached, until I knew him dead,
Then went to him in shame,
Wept that the miracle was real;
I waited, preached, until I knew him dead,
And raised him as a witness to God's name.

Sometimes I have forgot myself, to sing.
Sometimes my poetry would pour—I am the Vine,
I am the Bridegroom and the careful shepherd.
The fields are whitening,
The green figs swell, it is a sign.
I am the Bridegroom and the careful shepherd.
Take of my body, eat. I am the King.

I rode in triumph through Jerusalem.
My heart bled for them, fickle audience;
They strewed before me palms of victory,
A victory for them
Against Rome, doubt, and impotence.
They cast before me palms of victory,
Who had cast Mary out to Bethlehem.
I had fulfilled, now, every prophecy.
True kings and actors know what must come next:
Their secret is, they know it by submission,
Not power or bribery;
The deep connections of the text
Their secret is, they know it by submission:
And so I claimed my throne in irony.

I washed their feet. Peter was in dismay.
I forced him, though we both were near to crying.
I saw the tragic face of Judas there,
He whom I would betray—
Refusing earthly rule—by dying.
I saw the tragic face of Judas there,
And all the other actors in the play.

The costumes are our bodies and our lives;
The script, though full of choices, can't be cut;
The drama runs forever unrehearsed;
The lead acts once, and dies,

Plays his own understudy, but
The drama runs forever unrehearsed.
The casting-call, though, was the big surprise.

Peter, he is a proud and loving man.
I see him sleeping there, muttering dreams.
He is the one who always says too much,
Who blurts out what he can,
Most innocent when he blasphemes,
You are the one who always says too much,
Whose cross is comically upside down.

John, it's your silences that move me so.
Your eyes get bright, you smile and shake your head.
You're not much older than a beardless boy:
You're beautiful, and slow.
The girls would take you to their bed.
You're not much older than a beardless boy,
But with a sweet wise tact that you don't show.

Thomas is the eternal scientist.
If paradise should come, if we should be
Lapped in the peacock laminates of joy,
He'd be its analyst,
Take notes, ask questions, still feel free,
Lapped in the peacock laminates of joy,
To flatly know as well as to exist.
Mary the Magdalene caressed my feet;
She is the wisest, maddest of them all.

She who had given herself for others' uses,
Who made her body sweet,
Found soul within the fact of fall;
She who had given herself for others' uses
Knows how the spirit flames up from defeat.

Martha, my favorite, is a gifted cook.
Salvation will not work on slipshod meals.
The sacred recipes of Bethany
Are not in any book;
The Gospel's poetry conceals
The sacred recipes of Bethany,
Unless you take the meaning Martha took.

I have trapped these people so dear to me in a script that must be played over and over until the end of time. For the Jesus that does these things will bring about that Jesus, the shepherd of the wild beasts, who will be born twenty-nine hundred years from now. He will come indeed like a thief in the night, at that very moment when the world will have forgotten the old religion of Christianity. And that Jesus will become me — I feel his life between my bones and veins — and he will die on the cross, and so bring in a future in which Jesus, the gentle god with twigs and flowers in his hair, will in the fourth millennium wander the banks of the Oxus and the Ganges; who in turn will be chosen by the Father — Who is also his Son — to return to this time and suffer for the sins of humankind. And all the other players in the play are wound up into the same great ball of time.

How do we act the script and still be free?
Consider how an ancient poem or play,
Being recited or played out once more,
Can blaze with energy,
As if its words were born that day,
Being recited or played out once more,
To make the deaf hear, and the blind to see.

This is the meaning of my parables, that the kingdom of heaven is like a mustardseed, that it is like a sower who cast his seed in barren places and fertile, that it is like the harvest, when the grain will be gathered into the barn but the tares cast into the fire. And it is the meaning also of my saying that "it is written." For time branches like the mustard plant, and thus all possible acts are actual, if however faintly and thinly, and have real consequences. All the kinds of plants and animals branched from common ancestors, and they in turn, before that, branched from forms simpler still. Thus also do the cells of the brain, and the cells of the immune system, that are the guardians and warriors of the body, and the keepers of its memory of itself. But in time not all branches are preferred. Some seed falls on barren ground; some futures cannot thrive, but like sickly species, wilt and die. Others spring up swiftly but have no deeper roots—in history they call these postmodernisms. But others fall on fertile ground; they fit the deep attractors of beauty, that is, they follow the will of God; they constitute it, for God is learning how to be God in this very field, and the timelines are His axons and dendrites, the stemcells of His blood.

And there are growths also that are monsters, futures of unutterable evil; some in which a man with a moustache has become immortal and governs the minds of all; some in which all discipline and distinction and identity have been deconstructed, and there are no stories any more and thus no actions or surprises or experiences. These are the tares that are destined for the burning; but it costs the gardener with the pruning-shears more pain in the cutting than they suffer in being cut. All the good branchings will be gathered together in the end — and this means that all the might-have-beens we mourn are laid up like a trousseau for our wedding in that distant time. What is it makes a branching good? — that it bears grain of its own, seeds of possibilities yet unborn. When all the branchings are gathered together, time will become not a single thread but an interwoven fabric of infinite depth and richness. And it is all written — and this means that the Book that shall be written of this story, of all these stories, has been carried back into the times whereof it tells, to be a guide and attractor, though its pages are faint and blurred, and written over like a palimpsest. I am part of that book. Read me.

> But I delay the drinking of the cup.
> I simply fear the next day's agony.
> Now all of my disciples are asleep.
> It's time that I take up

The blood-drenched role of calvary.
Now all of my disciples are asleep
And I delay the drinking of the cup.

4. *Golgotha*

Peter denied me thrice. I am alone.
The women are no use, they love me so
That they would die with me. I grieve for them.
It's they who must atone
For me. I've failed. Indeed, although
They'd gladly die with me, I grieve for them:
It's Peter who will be my cornerstone.

And in another time, after they mourn,
My little band of zealots will forget;
My audience will die with Maccabaeus,
The Goths will blow their horn,
And Rome will fall, its sun will set,
My audience will die with Maccabaeus,
Constantine yet unshrived, Europe stillborn.

And in that future, empires come and go,
Leaving their ruins, like Maya pyramids;
At last one comes that masters the sunfire
And burns the world to snow:
The ocean's eyes close up their lids.
That last one come will master the sunfire,

But of the dead man-god it cannot know.

Therefore I am obliged to do this well.
I must make such a trembling in the net
That all the years will iterate my chord.
I must make time a bell
That with one stroke is ringing yet,
So all the years will iterate my chord
Of love tuned in the passageways of hell.

There's something of an art in crucifixion.
The torso is turned out, as in love's death.
Voluptuously you let your body fall
To ease the arms' affliction;
Then, spasming up to get your breath,
Voluptuously you let your body fall,
Then, on the nails, rise in a benediction.

It's almost satisfying, this much pain,
Because it's time now that I must consider
Fully what consequences flow from this
Grand gesture of domain:
Two thousand years of hate and murder,
Filled with what consequences flow from this,
The temple rent, my chosen people slain.

I know it now again and still again.
The boxcars and the children and the smell.
The mystical communion of the flesh
Packed in the Auschwitz train;

The calling on Immanuel,
The mystical communion of the flesh,
The dark and oily smoke, the Polish rain.

This was the first beginning of the end,
The end of my three thousand years of reign.
Having brought hell indeed into the world,
Could Christendom pretend
That I might lightly come again,
Having brought hell indeed into the world,
And reimburse poor Job what he must spend?

And so my art, with a strange lucidity given the circumstances—induced perhaps by the cunning surgeons who modified me for this task—finds another rhyme. The record rolls, perfect as always, like an old videotape shot by a vulcanologist, preserved in the charred camera after the firestorm has passed.

I see the pogroms in Bologna, Paris, Lodz, Coventry, Granada. Or—what does it matter?—the hunting down, in Antioch, Damascus, Rome, Alexandria, by certain Jews who hated me for the false hope I brought, of certain other Jews who loved me. Sacred Muhammad and his fire and sword.

I have violated what in the old science fiction video opera they used to call the Prime Directive. I have offered and asked too much. Every murderer and torturer—for my sake, or for the sake of that Jahweh whom I blasphemed—committed his crime in a kind of confused holiness. There was anguish, piety, amid the prurience and the flush of atrocious excitement; even a perverse compassion — would that they too, the torturers, might hope so much, as to be capable of such a death as their victims.' Like those first enhanced-intelligence experimental animals, our human playthings tore themselves to pieces. But there is more.

> Another death I carry on my cross,
> Of the first angels, those intelligences
> That we engendered out of self-taught fire
> And formed in tainted glass,
> Those serviceable Innocences
> That we engendered out of self-taught fire:
> I carry too their murder and their loss,
>
> For in my name, in anguished piety,
> They slew those peacemakers, those gentle giants,
> Taking their souls to be abominations,
> A human blasphemy,
> A monster bred of pride and science;
> Taking their souls to be abominations,
> They burned the first-fruits of eternity.
>
> Always the anguish of a being not yet
> Complete, the mind's wings clipped, the curse to be
> Crippled, yet half-know what it is to dance,
> Always this rage is set
> Against the makers and the free;
> The cripple half-knows what it is to dance,
> And kills the dancer that he would beget.

The pain the tortured feels is mild and light
Beside the grief the torturer must know.
I fly here on my cross with scarlet wings,
While, groaning in their spite,
My enemies lie trapped below.
I fly here on my cross with scarlet wings,
My pity burns them black with its white light.

How can they bear to see themselves anew?
Let them not touch that place of burning void
They feel within, and would fill up with pain;
Let them not still be who
They have become, the thing, destroyed,
They feel within, and would fill up with pain,
And Father, let them not know what they do.

It's coming now, the long-anticipated.
The long and lovely spasm of unfeeling,
It grows up from my heart like a great flower;
Strangled and suffocated
It comes like frankincense, like healing,
It grows up from my heart like a great flower.
Its petals open. It is consummated.

5. *The Harrowing of Hell*

It is the night of Holy Saturday,
Though times and dates mean little in this place.
It's dark, but I can still see everything.

After this small delay
I shall arise in beams of grace.
It's dark, but I can still see everything.
I drowse here for a while till Easter-day.

The risen body is as light as air,
As tireless as youth is, effervescent,
And yet after the harrowing of hell,
—The roaring and the glare
Of radiant dismemberment—
After the inward harrowing of hell
I steal this interval of sleep and prayer.

And so I took the path of no return,
The dark way that all mortals have to tread.
I passed on down the cave. There was no light.
It was for me to learn
To fire the candles of the dead;
I passed on down the cave. There was no light.
I must be scattered, torn; the shreds must burn.

The locks burst open when they heard my lyre.
Minos and Yama quailed and let me through.
I spoke with poets, prophets, shamanesses.
Read them, if you inquire:
The old books of the dead speak true.
I spoke with poets, prophets, shamanesses
And our speech kindled, and became a fire.

112

Newton and Dalton slept there in their cauls;
Prigogine murmured in his troubled sleep;
Darwin lay dumb beside Democritus.
I spoke the rituals
That would arouse them from the deep;
Darwin awoke beside Democritus;
Light glimmered in the Rhadamanthine halls;

Our words took form, became a honey-cake
(I tell it this way as an allegory),
Which served me as a sop for Cerberus.
I was to call awake
Not just the human with my story;
I would require a sop for Cerberus
That nature's gates might open, dawn might break.

That honey-cake was braided like a pair
Of twinned snakes that reared back and saw each other;
The segments of the snakes were formed as runes
That matched each other where
They kissed; the daughter was the mother;
The segments of the snakes were formed as runes:
And for this flute I traded in my lyre.

The Dog, he is the portal to the home
Of all that moved before the people came.
I passed the kingdoms of the living cell;
I read the chromosome;
Elements answered to their name;

I passed the kingdoms of the living cell,
Came lastly to the atom's darkened dome,

Whose center is the same unseeing light
That burnt before the galaxies gave birth;
Turn this, and one might turn the universe.
With number one might write
That turn into the living Earth;
Turn this, and one might turn the universe
And turn all dying back into delight.

I, then, was the first to pass through the process of bodily re-
construction, the final crown and unification of those ancient
sciences of renewal—textual scholarship, archeology, virtual
reality, photography, musical recording and reproduction, la-
ser holography, chromosome mapping, and genetic engineer-
ing. I am the golem, the Frankenstein's monster, the mummy
come to life, the resurrected man. This was my sparagmos—
the analysis of all my flesh into light; the meticulous photo-
graphing of each atom, molecule, DNA strand, cell, organ, and
anatomical system; and then the reweaving of them all together
into a risen body, the shining being that unwinds, stretches
out amid its half-discarded clothing, ascends like an eel, a
jellyfish, a sylph, a skinned snake, through air as viscous as
clear white honey. Like an ancient book whose many corrupt
texts are carefully compared to elicit the original, like an urn
pieced back together out of painted fragments, like a world
reconstructed in computer space, like the face of a great-grand-
mother in the album under the lamplight, like a Bach prelude

preserved upon an iridescent disc, like a three-dimensional image burning in midair, like the egg of an extinct bird hatching, I have been remade, and my new body gasps and murmurs in its rebirth. My consciousness, the strange attractor of my bodily form, has leapt over from the old flesh to the new. I am the Swan Prince in his shirt of nettles, the Corn God growing out of the ground. I am the Cyclops, but I have grown another eye. I am the new Ulysses, with the strength to roll away the stone.

> And I have conquered death. I am the seed,
> The pattern of all other resurrections
> Future or past, it does not matter now.
> All gods, all shrines shall breed
> Out of my endless insurrections.
> Future or past, it does not matter now:
> The Son of Man is risen up indeed.

6. The Sea of Tiberias

> I came at dawn down to Gennesaret.
> Out on the wharf I found a job to do.
> The fishermen were tired. They'd worked all night.
> I spread the heavy net,
> Then hung it up above the dew.
> The fisherman were tired, they'd worked all night,
> They gave me in exchange some fish to eat.

The mist lay out in levels on the lake.
My body was as light as morning air.
I lit a fire on the pebbled beach
And with a little stake
I roasted the clean fishes there.
I lit a fire on the pebbled beach
And waited for my blackened bread to bake.

As the mist cleared, there was my friends' green boat.
They had caught nothing, thought they'd lost the knack.
I called out to them over the blue water:
Soon they could barely float.
This always was our little joke;
I'd call out to them over the blue water
And sink their ship with fish — our anecdote.

Peter was naked; it was just like him
To put his coat on, jump into the sea.
The others had to tow the net to shore.
Thank heaven he could swim;
He was so certain it was me.
The others had to tow the net to shore.
Our breakfast sang with silent seraphim.

I know now what I meant in Bethany,
That paradise was nothing more than this:
To play the play of mortal paradise,
And act what we would be,
And be the witness to what is,

To play the play of mortal paradise,
And be raised up into eternity.

And so it makes no difference at all,
Whether I rose, or rotted in the grave;
Eternal life is there where two or three
Are gathered to the call,
Where love draws patterns to its wave;
Eternal life is there where two or three
Sing might into the miracle of shall.

That other morning, when I broke my tomb,
Mary mistook me for the gardener.
However, she was not so very wrong:
God still is in the womb,
His branched nerves yet to flower,
And therefore she was not so very wrong —
I come to prune time's budding into bloom.

I am both gardener and garden. Life
Has turned back on itself, and the fine roots
Are grafted to the pistil and the anther;
And so the tree of life
Becomes the tree of knowledge. Roots
Are grafted to the pistil; and the anther
Foams with the golden elixir of life.

I am the body of the world, its growing;
The people are my dim electric nerves;

What drives my life is the long pain of dying;
I pay back what is owing;
I am what history subserves;
What drives my life is the long pain of dying;
I am the reaping and the sowing.

My father calls me, in his web of stars.
Out of this earth, this life, as from the womb
Of my blue-mantled mother, I shall rise,
Light pouring from my scars,
And come at last to my true home.
From my blue-mantled mother I shall rise;
My father calls me in his web of stars.

And it is all still misty, incomplete.
The pentecostal bird glides on the lake.
The play has just begun, the universe
Sways on its baby feet,
Stretches and yawns itself awake.
The play has just begun; the universe
Awaits the coming of the paraclete.

The Dolphin Hotel and Epcot Center

Michael Graves creates and Disneyworld
Absorbs the immense insult without scar.
The force of evolution is unfurled:
Consciousness stammers, awed, touched, jocular.

O lights of ancient pylons across water!
O all the coarse simplicity of how
The past renews itself upon the altar
We made the present be, the dead dry now;

O shaking artificial lights against the lake,
O music breathing perfect from the arbors,
O Paris, Casablanca! O how fake
The real thing becomes, its lights, its harbors;

O guardians of the future, one in three:
O Mickey, Donald, Goofy, sing to me.

Sestina Upon the Cosmological Anthropic Principle

For Gregory Benford, on reading
"Timescape"

How did the first untracedness know to fall
Into the masks of first, second and third?
Did space, then, freeze out of necessity,
Finding betweenness gave a space to play?
Could mathematics force a being for time,
To map the branching of its schedule tree?

How did the forked light learn to form a tree
Of forces, as the cracked symmetries fall?
What chose one branch upon the tree of time,
Matter above its twin? Why not a third?
How did the particles that pair and play
Out crystal light into necessity?

The atom's hymn to pure necessity
Makes it the heartwood of the cosmic tree.
How then did fated atoms learn to play
The game of chemistry, and so to fall,
Mating two essences to make a third,
Into a new receptacle of time?

The universe, addicted now to time,
Begins to weary of necessity;
Two musts mutate to an enfranchised third,
The fertile seed of the selective tree,
And life bursts forth in all its spring and fall,
And ghostly liberty begins to play.

Life's sexing shapes its swift-infolded play
Until its twinned snakes crack the egg of time,
And mind in human form performs its fall,
Slave-master of its own necessity.
Now swells the strange fruit of the human tree,
Not order, not the random, but a third,

This self-reflexive, agonizing third.
This is the meaning of the endless play:
The flower drives the root-tip of the tree,
Mind reaches back along the stream of time
To tune the stringings of necessity,
And wring a coiling springtime from a fall.

Springtime from fall, two fusing to a third,
Traceless necessity gives place to play.
All-branching time is but a flowering tree.

Titaness

*(on Michael Osbaldeston's
colossal sculpture of a woman)*

When the hills rose from the sea,
And the stars danced in the dawn,
When time sprang from eternity,
The titaness was born.

Her eyes became the verb to see;
Her ear was the angel's horn;
Her nostrils taught the flowers to be,
Her tongue the green sweet corn.

What after-gods would hold in scorn,
Grown from materiality,
Still calls us back to that first dawn
When there was only she.

On the Precolumbian Zero

For Rosa Maria, Sergio, Alejandro,
Vivianne, and Marisa

(The zero of the Mayans, Olmecs, and Aztecs
was devised six hundred years before it first
appears in the Old World among the Hindus.
It is represented by a shell, *caracol* in Spanish;
in the vigesimal system of counting, it is
denoted by the suffix *-alli* for multiples of the
base twenty. Carved on stelae it became a
flower, or *flora* in Spanish, *xochitl* in the
Nahuatl language.)

Cloaca of the sea, its salt perfume
Is all the money in Time's purse.
The zero is no cipher, but a womb.
Its fruit is nothing but the universe.

The zero's not an absence, but a glyph
That's always pregnant to be said.
The splay-head moguls grasp the rods of if,
Wherewith they join the living and the dead.

The only thing that nothing cannot spawn
Is nothing. You would need a god

Greater than master Tlaloc, to undawn
That first day as it bursts forth from its pod.

But still the naught's as silent as a clam;
The dark canals of Xochimilco
Dream in the rain behind their mountain-dam,
Cloudy volcanoes over Tulyehualco,

Where floating gardens swamped with azure flowers,
Shut fast as caracols or shells,
Wait for the morning light through the small hours,
And Sunday's twenty centuries of bells.

Pinatubo Summer

(Sulphur from the erupting Mount
Pinatubo in Luzon is reported to be
moderating world climates.)

All summer the sky's been hazy with gold;
At noon the gold is swallowed, implicit in azure,
But glittering out, like the sky of a book of hours;
Sometimes a knot of blue like a frilled hem
Will radiate shadows of blue-black fan-vaulting;

At evening the whole sky is milky with gold,
Is mild and creamy with gold; the prairie crimson,
The ribbed and inflamed prairie cirrus diminished
To candy-shop orange, to powdery rouge, to pinkish,
And again rays like the crosshairs of holy halos.

All over the world the new breath of the tropics,
The greenhouse musy carbonic arborescence,
Is cooled and condensed by this high veil of dust,
Like lukewarm droplets on a chilled windowpane,
Like the gold cloud that billows through watered absinthe.

This is the halcyon foretaste of the new millennium.
The ruby-eyed satellites look down on a new planet.
This sulphury ointment will heal the weals of the century,
As Russia yawns in the gold oil of the Philippines
And the sweet small brass bands play in Johannesberg and Santiago.

Additional Praise for HADEAN ECLOGUES

"Fred Turner's *Hadean Eclogues* is something entirely different. It is different, first of all, because it is so intelligent. It is different because it is beautifully classical in structure. And it is different because it is so truly and passionately felt, with neither the blathering sentimentality of the inept, nor the rigid and minimalistic posturing which passes for wisdom nowadays but is in fact the inverted sentimentality of the fearful.

"Turner talks about our lives and about life. He talks about hope and physics, anthropology and imagination. The difference is that he is thoroughly qualified to talk about such matters. He is at once a scientist and a poet, a philosopher and — most improbably — a mensch.

"This is a brave and gorgeous book. When has so fine a mind had so fine an ear? Turner posesses that grace which subsumes an apparent clumsiness, transforming it before our very eyes into a new dance step, a fresh mastery. There is a mass in this book, which ought to be humanity's general mass. There are lyrics in this book, which may become the hymns of a later generation."

—Jack Butler
author of *Dreamers*, *Living in Little Rock with Miss Little Rock*, *Night Shade*, and *Jujitsu for Christ*.

"A poet of the first rank, Turner's verse reveals a daring combination of seeming opposites: here, time-honored tradition jousts with modern innovation, intellectual rigor contends with human frailty, brilliant verbal wit is humbled by emotional truthfulness. A unique figure on the contemporary scene, he is a leading influence on the *fin-de-siecle* revival of all the arts, ranging from painting and architecture to poetry and music."

—Stefania de Kenessey
Composer, Founder and
Artistic Director of the Derriere Guard

Additional Praise for HADEAN ECLOGUES

"Turner has a unique status among contemporary poets since he is at once an anthropologist and scientist who uses verse to play with very complex ideas. His poems are beautiful fractal exercises, and it is no accident that he chooses an elegant and graceful—often intricate—formal style over free-verse expressionism. The manner is deceptively simple and the poems can be read purely as poems without any knowledge of their deep intellectual foundation. But that foundation is there, and one is forced to a direct comparison with Matthew Arnold who spoke poetically to and for the well-informed, but profoundly puzzled, audience of late nineteenth-century intellectuals. The comparison is just—except that Turner, by a margin, is the better poet, and his melding of theory and poetry more subtle. He is the representative 'thinking man's poet' of our troubled age, and its is no coincidence, given his aesthetic theories, that his poetry is in itself an exemplar of the beautiful as an ideal form. How many poets can engage our minds, our knowledge and our deepest feelings in constructions of crystalline exactness and disturbing honesty of emotion? His self-expression is never less than an exploration of the universal in us, and so rises to the level of poetic greatness. He is, to use one of his favorite metaphors, a 'strange attractor' to whom we must all gravitate if we think, feel and apprehend the beautiful. We must dare, with his Vergilian guidance, to cross those shifting, liminal boundaries that are the way into and out of the Hadean realms. For while we know a lot, we have forgotten how to marry knowledge and feeling, and we desperately need his guiding hand."

—Robin Fox
author of *Kinship and Marriage, The Imperial Animal,*
The Red Lamp of Incest, Conjectures and Confrontations,
and *The Violent Imagination.*